FOREST

Sean Callery

Consultant: David Burnie

KINGFISHER

NEW YORK

KINGFISHER
LONDON & NEW YORK

Copyright © Kingfisher 2012
Published in the United States by Kingfisher,
175 Fifth Ave., New York, NY 10010
Kingfisher is an imprint of Macmillan Children's Books, London.
All rights reserved.

Distributed in the U.S. and Canada by Macmillan, 175 Fifth Ave., New York, NY 10010

Library of Congress Cataloging-in-Publication data has been applied for.

ISBN: 978-0-7534-6741-1

Kingfisher books are available for special promotions and premiums.
For details contact: Special Markets Department, Macmillan,
175 Fifth Ave., New York, NY 10010.

For more information, please visit www.kingfisherbooks.com

Printed in China
1 3 5 7 9 8 6 4 2
1TR/1211/WKT/UNTD/140MA

Note to readers: the website addresses listed in this book are correct at
the time of going to print. However, due to the ever-changing nature
of the Internet, website addresses and content can change. Websites
can contain links that are unsuitable for children. The publisher cannot
be held responsible for changes in website addresses or content or for
information obtained through a third party. We strongly advise that
Internet searches be supervised by an adult.

The publisher would like to thank the following for permission to reproduce their material. Every care has been taken to trace copyright holders. However,
if there have been unintentional omissions or failure to trace copyright holders, we apologize and will, if informed, endeavor to make corrections in any future edition.
top = t; bottom = b; center = c; left = l; right = r

All artwork Stuart Jackson-Carter (Peter Kavanagh Art Agency)

Cover main Shutterstock/Sam DCruz; cover tl Naturepl/Tom Vezo; cover tcl Naturepl/Rolf Nussbaumer; cover tcr Shutterstock/Tony Campbell; cover tr Frank Lane Picture Agency
(FLPA)/Mark Raycroft; back cover t Shutterstock/Monica Ottino; back cover c Shutterstock/Geanina Bechea; back cover bl Shutterstock/Noah Strycker; back cover cb Shutterstock/
J. Y. Page 1 Shutterstock/mashe; 2 Shutterstock/Marek R. Swadzba; 3t Shutterstock/Mclek; 3b Shutterstock/Henk Bentlage; 4tr Shutterstock/viscerailimage; 4bl Shutterstock/
godrick; 4br Shutterstock/Radka Palenikova; 5tl Shutterstock/Ronnie Howard; 5tr Shutterstock/ethylalkohol; 5bc Shutterstock/YK; 5br Shutterstock/Volodymyr Burdiak; 6tr
Shutterstock/Andrea J. Smith; 6bl Science Photo Library (SPL)/Darwin Dale; 6br Photolibrary/Imagebroker; 7tl Photolibrary/Bios; 7tr Shutterstock/photolinc; 7ct Photolibrary/OSF; 7c
Shutterstock/MindStorm; 7cb SPL/George Bernard; 7bl Photolibrary/OSF; 7br Shutterstock/aopsan; 7br Shutterstock/Olga Mishyna; 7br Shutterstock/Sergielev; 8bl Shutterstock/Roger
Meerts; 9tl Shutterstock/kurt_G; 9tc Shutterstock/Mark R. Swadzba; 9tr Shutterstock/Le Do; 9ct Shutterstock/kurt_G; 9c Shutterstock/Roger Meerts; 9cb Shutterstock/kurt_G; 9br
Shutterstock/Le Do; 9br Shutterstock/zshunfa; 9br Shutterstock/Stephen van Horn; 9br Shutterstock/Richard Griffin; 10tr FLPA/Cyril Russo/Minden; 10bl Nature/Bernard Castelein;
10br Photolibrary/Dhritiman Mukherjee; 11tl Nature/Bernard Castelein; 11tr Shutterstock/Swapan; 11c FLPA/Ingo Arndt/Minden; 11br Shutterstock/hans.slegers; 12tr
Photolibrary/White; 12bl Photoshot/Andy Rouse; 12br Photolibrary/Animals Animals; 13tl Photolibrary/Juniors Bildarchiv; 13tr Shutterstock/konmesa; 13ct Alamy/Juniors
Bildarchiv; 13c Shutterstock/Chris Sargent; 13cb Shutterstock/dean bertoncelj; 13bl Naturepl/E. A. Kuttapan; 13br Shutterstock/Noah Strycker; 13br Shutterstock/J. Y.; 13br
Shutterstock/Kristina Stasiuliene; 14tr FLPA/Mark Raycroft/Minden; 14bl Naturepl/Arco; 14br Naturepl/Tom Vezo; 15tl Naturepl/Rolf Nussbaumer; 15tr Shutterstock/Chantal de
Bruijne; 15ct Photolibrary/Peter Arnold Images; 15c Shutterstock/Tony Campbell; 15cb Shutterstock/Rusty Dodson; 15bl Naturepl/Rolf Nussbaumer; 15br Shutterstock/Karin
Jaehne; 15br Shutterstock/Hintau Aliaksei; 16bl FLPA/Frank W. Lane; 17tl Photolibrary/Animals Animals; 17tr Shutterstock/Marco Uliana; 17ct Naturepl/Barry Mansell; 17cb
Naturepl/Barry Mansell; 17br Shutterstock/Henrik Larsson; 17br Shutterstock/Rob Byron; 17br Shutterstock/Reinhold Leitner; 17br Shutterstock/Alessandro Zocc; 18tr Shutterstock/
Takahashi Photography; 18bl Alamy/Allen Thornton; 18br Naturepl/Roger Powell; 19tl Naturepl/Philip Dalton; 19tr Shutterstock/Arto Hakola; 19ct Shutterstock/jadimages; 19cb
Shutterstock/mlorenz; 19bl FLPA/Ron Austing; 19br Shutterstock/Steve Byland; 19br Shutterstock/R. Gino Santa Maria; 19br Shutterstock/Mike Truchon; 19br Shutterstock/
mlorenz; 20bl with the very kind permission of Mr. Paul D. Brock, Scientific Associate of the Natural History Museum, London; 21tr Shutterstock/Gerrit_de_Vries; 21cb Shutterstock/
kurt_G; 21br Shutterstock/Tamara Kulikova; 21br Shutterstock/bloom; 22tr Naturepl/Jouan & Ruis; 22bl Photoshot/NHPA; 22br Markus Grimm; 23tl Naturepl/Pete Oxford; 23tr
Shutterstock/Willem Bosman; 23c Shutterstock/Mogens Trolle; 23cb Photolibrary/Mike Hill; 23bl Photolibrary/Hoberman Collection U.K.; 23br Shutterstock/Maria Gioberti; 24tr
Naturepl/Tim Laman; 24bl FLPA/Shem Compion; 24br Naturepl/Tim Laman; 25tl Photolibrary/OSF; 25tr Shutterstock/Cre8tive Images; 25ct FLPA/Andrew Forsyth; 25c FLPA/
David Tipling; 25cb FLPA/Michael Krabs/Imagebroker; 25bl Naturepl/Patricia Robles Gil; 25br Shutterstock/Fedor Selivanov; 25br Shutterstock/Tamara Kulikova; 25br Shutterstock/
Leah-Anne Thompson; 26tr Photoshot/NHPA; 26bl Shutterstock/Chris Kruger; 26br FLPA/Suzi Esterhas/Minden; 27tl Naturepl/Ingo Arndt; 27tr Shutterstock/Sue Robinson; 27c
Shutterstock/Mogens Trolle; 27cb Photoshot/NHPA; 27bl FLPA/Suzi Esterhas/Minden; 27br Shutterstock/Andrejs Pidjass; 27br Shutterstock/Tamara Kulikova; 27br Shutterstock/
Francois van Heerden; 27br Shutterstock/Ultrashock; 30tl Shutterstock/Steve Byland; 30tr Shutterstock/Johan Swanepoel; 30bl Shutterstock/Peter Gyure; 30br Shutterstock/
Setaphong Tantanawat; 31tl Shutterstock/Geanina Bechea; 31tr Shutterstock/Monica Ottino; 31bl Shutterstock/Worakit Sirijinda; 31br Shutterstock/Tomas Sereda; 32tl
Shutterstock/Mike Truchon; 32br Shutterstock/Margaret M. Stewart

Contents

Introduction 4

Forests of southern Asia
Honeybee 6
White crab spider 8
Gray langur 10
Bengal tiger 12

Forests of North America
White-tailed deer 14
Vampire bat 16
Red-tailed hawk 18

Forests of southern Africa
Stick insect 20
Chameleon 22
Hornbill 24
Wild dog 26

A food web from southern Asia 28
Glossary and websites 30
Index 32

Introduction

Temperate forests are full of trees, plants, and animals. The weather can be hot or cold, and there are four seasons in a year, unlike in rainforests, where it is always summer.

All living things have to eat to stay alive. Some make their own food, some eat plants, and many try to eat one another. The list of who eats who is called a food chain.

Many animals eat trees and plants. Pill bugs, for example, eat rotting wood. Rabbits eat roots and leaves. Animals like these are next in a food chain and are called primary consumers.

NORTH AMERICA

food chain 2

equator

SOUTH AMERICA

Most food chains start with things that make their own food using the Sun's energy. Plants and trees do this. They are called producers.

Animals known as secondary consumers come next. They eat other animals. Chimpanzees, for example, eat insects and rodents.

This book takes you through three food chains in temperate forests around the world. You will find out about the life cycles of 11 animals: how they are born, grow, reproduce, and die.

EUROPE

ASIA

food chain 1

AFRICA

ood chain 3 __

AUSTRALIA

At the top of a food chain is a predator, such as a lynx. It is safe from attack once it is an adult because it is bigger, faster, or fiercer than the other creatures in its habitat.

Honeybee

The eastern honeybee lives in the forests of southern Asia. It collects nectar from flowers and turns it into honey. Bees do a special dance to guide one another to the best nectar.

1 A queen bee leaves her nest, taking thousands of bees with her. They build a new nest, and she lays an egg in each cell of the waxy honeycombs.

2 After three days, larvae hatch from the eggs. Worker bees feed them a special jelly and then later honey and pollen. They will shed their skin five times as they grow.

4 After another nine days, adult bees chew their way out of the cells. Most adults are female worker bees, but there are also males and new queen bees.

3 Five days later, the larvae spin silk cocoons around themselves and start to change into pupae. Worker bees seal them in their cells with caps of wax.

Did you know?

A honeybee picks up pollen from flowers on its hairy body. When it visits other flowers, the pollen rubs off. This helps plants reproduce.

Bees have two pairs of wings. The buzzing noise that they make is the sound of their wings flapping thousands of times every minute.

A bee's stinger contains venom. It stays in the animal that the bee has stung. The bee usually dies soon after stinging.

Queen bees live for five years, but other types of bees do not live as long. Sometimes there is more than nectar inside a flower . . .

White crab spider

This cunning spider does not spin a web to catch its prey. Instead, it sits on a flower and waits, hidden by the petals. Bees do not see it until it is too late and the spider pounces.

1 The female weaves an egg sac made of silk on a leaf. Males try to mate with her, but they are much smaller than she is, and sometimes they get eaten!

2 The female lays about 45 fertilized eggs in the egg sac. She stays there guarding the sac from predators and does not eat.

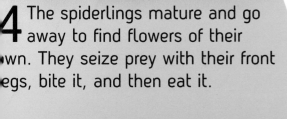

4 The spiderlings mature and go away to find flowers of their own. They seize prey with their front legs, bite it, and then eat it.

3 The eggs hatch into spiderlings. The mother guards and feeds them with prey such as bees, wasps, and other insects. She may be eaten herself if food is in short supply.

Did you know?

Spiders have two large eyes set on little growths called tubercles on the front of their head.

The white crab spider is named after its curved, clawlike legs and flat body. It can also move sideways like a crab.

The spider's fangs carry strong venom that paralyzes prey. The spider can then suck out its victim's insides.

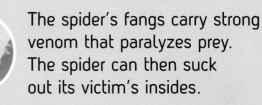

White crab spiders live for two years unless an animal eats the flowers on which they sit and swallows them, too . . .

Gray langur

Gray langurs are very sociable monkeys that live in large groups. Their diet is mainly fruit, flowers, and leaves. When food is in short supply, they eat spiders and insects.

1 The female gives birth to one or sometimes two babies between January and June. The tiny infants cling to their mothers for the first week of life.

2 A baby monkey suckles milk from its mother and from other females in the colony. It is fully weaned after about a year.

4 Langur groups can contain 10–60 monkeys. Females stay [i]n the group they were born into, but [m]ales leave. Langurs spend a lot of [ti]me on the ground but sleep in trees.

3 The baby can run and jump from the age of two months. Soon it [s]tarts to find its own food, learns to [c]limb in the branches, and walks [o]n the ground on four legs.

Did you know?

Did you know?

 Langurs have very good eyesight. The group always has a lookout high up in the treetops to spot danger.

Langurs are noisy all the time and use a variety of calls, from loud screams of alarm to gentle grunts and rumbles.

A langur's big toe is long and flexible like a thumb. It is used for climbing and holding the leaves that make up most of the monkey's diet.

Langur monkeys can live for 20 years as long as they do not meet an animal that roams the forest and climbs trees . . .

Bengal tiger

Tigers lurk in the forest shadows, stalking deer, monkeys, and other prey. Their stripes keep them hidden until it is time to pounce. Then there is no escape for the prey.

1 Every two to three years, the female produces a litter of up to four cubs. She will give birth in the shelter of a cave or a thick bush about four months after mating.

2 The cubs are born helpless and blind, but they soon find their place in the litter. One will boss the others around, taking their food for itself if there is not enough for all of them.

4 Tigers live alone from about the age of two. They can run, jump, climb trees, and swim, and they are the top predator in their territory.

3 The cubs begin to eat solid food at two months old but still suckle for up to six months. By then, they are able to follow their mother on hunting trips.

Did you know?

Tigers have claws that pull back into their paws. They sharpen them on trees, leaving scratches that mark their territory.

Tigers have large canine teeth and powerful jaws. They usually kill by squeezing the prey's throat until it cannot breathe any more.

A tiger's tongue is rough so it can scrape every last piece of meat from the bones of its prey.

Adult tigers live for 15–20 years because no other animals attack them. However, many tiger cubs are killed by adult male tigers.

White-tailed deer

White-tailed deer roam the forests of North America. They wander alone and in herds, eating the leaves, grasses, fruit, and plants that grow among the trees.

1 Males, called bucks, use their antlers to fight for the right to mate with a female. This happens during what is called the rutting season. Males rarely eat at this time.

2 Seven months after mating, the female gives birth to up to three fawns. They lie still and hide in the undergrowth for about a month, camouflaged by their spotted fur.

4 The fawns lose their spots during their first summer. Their stomachs are fully grown now, with four chambers that help them digest tough, leafy food.

3 The milk that young fawns suckle from their mothers contains a lot of fat and protein to help them grow. They start to search for solid food, too.

Did you know?

The deer lifts its tail and shows the white underside when it senses danger. This is where its name comes from.

Males grow antlers each year. The larger its antlers, the more likely a deer is to win fights and breed successfully.

The deer's large ears pick up the slightest sound of an approaching predator so that it can escape to safety.

Deer can run away from their predators, but one animal drinks their blood as they sleep . . .

Vampire bat

Vampire bats drink blood from mammals, such as pigs and deer. It is their only food. This does not harm the animal unless the bat is carrying a deadly disease called rabies.

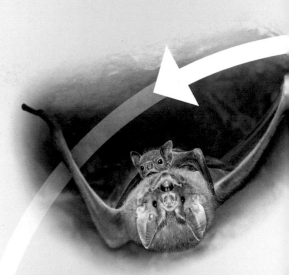

1 A female bat mates with a male in her colony during the breeding season. About six months later, she gives birth to a tiny baby.

2 Bats are mammals, so the infant suckles milk from its mother. It will do this for nine months, until it reaches adult size and weight.

Did you know?

A bat's wing has long fingers joined by a web of thin skin. The skin can rip but will heal itself.

Vampire bats make high-pitched sounds and listen for an echo. That tells them where trees are so that they do not fly into them in the dark.

Special sensors in a vampire bat's nose test the temperature around it and help the bat find its warm-blooded prey.

4 Vampire bat colonies live, or roost, in hollow trees and aves. Adults feed at night, biting nto the flesh of sleeping animals nd lapping up the blood that lows from the wounds.

3 If the mother dies, other bats take care of the orphaned oungster. Vampire bats feed ne another blood from mouth o mouth if food s scarce.

Vampire bats live for about nine years. Some predators with sharp eyesight can spot them flying at dusk . . .

Red-tailed hawk

Red-tailed hawks are killing machines in the sky, with excellent eyesight and sharp claws. They swoop down to catch prey, such as mice, on the ground and can grab a bat in midair with ease.

1 These hawks mate for life. They build wide, flat nests made of sticks and leaves 16–65 feet (5–20m) up a large tree. A pair uses the same nest each year.

2 The female lays one to three eggs in March or April. Most of the time, it is she who keeps them warm while the male hunts for food for her.

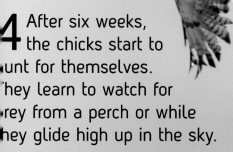

4 After six weeks, the chicks start to hunt for themselves. They learn to watch for prey from a perch or while they glide high up in the sky.

3 After a month, the eggs hatch into helpless chicks. The male brings food to the nest, and the female tears it into small pieces for the chicks. They gulp down as much as they can.

Did you know?

A short, hooked beak allows hawks to tear food into chunks that are small enough for them and their chicks to eat.

Hawks can see small animals at a distance of about half a mile (1km). A ridge of bone over each eye acts as a sunshade.

Hawks' feet have three toes at the front and one at the back. They are ideal for gripping prey.

Red-tailed hawks are at the top of their food chain. If they survive to become adults, they can live for 20 years.

Stick insect

Thunberg's stick insects look just like the plants they live on in the forests of southern Africa. They sit very still, hidden in the leaves for most of the day. They move around and eat at night.

1 Females drop their eggs on the ground. The brown, oval eggs look like plant seeds, so stick insects are camouflaged in their habitat even before they are born!

2 After four to six months, the eggs hatch into nymphs, which look like tiny adults. They climb a tree or plant to find food and shelter.

4 If they are threatened, adults can spray a clear liquid out of their mouths. It has a strong smell and can make a predator itch.

3 The nymphs shed their skin five times over the next six months. If a limb is lost or damaged, it is replaced during molting.

Did you know?

Stick insects have two antennae covered with tiny hairs. They pick up changes in the temperature and smells in the air.

This stick insect can grow up to 2.2 inches (56mm) long. It eats a lot of tough leaves and needs large, strong mouthparts.

A stick insect's feet have two claws and four suction pads to help the insect climb slippery surfaces such as plant stalks.

Stick insects live for about four months, but one false move can put them in danger from a sharp-sighted predator . . .

Chameleon

Flap-necked chameleons eat small creatures, such as flies and stick insects. Chameleons change color to scare their predators and to attract a mate—not to hide.

1 After mating, the female chameleon digs a hole in damp soil close to a tree and lays a clutch of 20–40 eggs. She covers them up and leaves them there.

2 Between nine and 12 months later, the babies bite their way out of the egg using a special tooth. The whole clutch will hatch within one week.

4 A chameleon catches food by flicking out its long, sticky tongue, which can stretch to the same length as its entire body.

3 Baby chameleons look like small adults. They start to hunt for food right away by climbing a tree and seeking out prey.

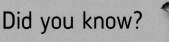

A chameleon can turn its eyes in different directions at the same time. This helps it escape from predators and spot prey.

Each foot has five toes that are connected to make a group of two and a group of three. This helps the chameleon grip onto thin branches.

The tail can curl around a branch, which helps the chameleon hold on tight as it climbs.

If they survive into adulthood, chameleons can live for two to three years, but they only move slowly and can be caught . . .

Hornbill

The southern ground hornbill is a large bird that eats chameleons and other reptiles, frogs, snails, and insects. It lives in groups, nesting in trees but spending most of its time on the ground.

1 Hornbills mate for life. Every few years, the female makes a nest in a hole in a tree, lining it with dry leaves. She lays one egg but may lay another one a week later.

2 The female keeps the eggs warm for 40 days while the male brings food. If there is not enough food, the first chick will be fed but the second will die.

4 Hornbills live in family groups of up to nine birds, led by a main pair. They hunt together and call out to one another when they have found food.

3 After about four months, the surviving chick can leave the nest, although most stay with their parents for some years. Hornbills can breed from the age of four.

Did you know?

Hornbills get their name from their long, curved beaks, which they use to spear and carry their food.

Their eyes are protected from the sun by long eyelashes. These are not hairs but a special type of feather.

The bird can inflate the skin around its throat like a balloon. The air inside vibrates to make the bird's call louder.

Hornbills can live for 50 years, but being on the ground most of the time can be dangerous . . .

Wild dog

African wild dogs hunt together in packs of about 20 animals. They will chase large prey, such as zebras, but also eat birds, especially injured ones that cannot fly away.

1 One female mates with the male pack leader. Ten weeks later, she gives birth to a litter of ten pups in an underground den.

2 The pups suckle milk from their mother for about three months. If their mother goes off to hunt befor they are old enough to go with her, other dogs will guard the pups.

Did you know?

A wild dog has large, round ears, which allow it to hear the calls of its pack far away. Dogs also lose heat through their ears when they get too hot.

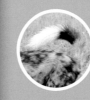

The wild dog's long, bushy tail has a white tip that acts like a flag and shows where pack members are during a hunt.

Wild dogs crush the bones of prey with their 42 teeth and strong jaws.

4 Females leave to join another pack and can mate after about a year. Males stay in the pack and may fight to be lead dog.

3 When the pack moves away from the den, all the dogs feed the pups by choking up, or regurgitating, food. The pups join in hunts after eight months.

Wild dogs live for about ten years. Besides lions, no other predators threaten the safety of the pack.

A food web from southern Asia

This book follows some forest food chains. Most animals eat more than one food, however, so they are part of several food chains. There are many food chains in the forests, and they link like a map to make a food web.

tiger

wild boar

golden eagle

gray langur

fairy bluebird

beetle

fruit

honeybee

crab
spider

Sun

plants

caterpillar

Glossary

ANTENNAE
A pair of feelers on an insect's head.

CAMOUFLAGE
To blend in with the surroundings and so avoid being seen easily.

CANINE TEETH
Special long, pointed teeth used for cutting through food.

CHAMBERS OF THE STOMACH
Some animals have several parts, or chambers, to their stomachs. This helps them digest tough leaves and grass.

COCOON
A hard outer case made by an insect, such as a bee, when it is changing into an adult.

COLONY
A group of the same kind of animal that lives together.

CONSUMER
A living thing that survives by eating other living things.

DEN
A wild animal's home.

FERTILIZE
When sperm from a male animal joins with the egg of a female to make a new life.

FLEXIBLE
Able to bend.

HABITAT
The natural home of an animal.

INFLATE
To fill with air.

LITTER
A group of baby animals born to the same mother.

MAMMAL
An animal that has fur and feeds milk to its young.

MATE
When a male and female animal reproduce. Some animals mate at a particular time each year called the mating season. For deer, this is called the rutting season.

MOLT
When an animal gets rid of the outside of its body. This is also called shedding.

NYMPH
A young insect that is not yet fully grown and has no wings.

ORPHAN
A young animal whose parents have died.

PACK
A group of the same kind of animal that lives and/or hunts together.

PARALYZE
To hurt an animal so that it cannot move.

PREDATOR
An animal that kills and eats other animals.

PRODUCER
A living thing, such as a plant, that makes its own food from the energy of the Sun.

RODENT
A gnawing animal, such as a rat or mouse.

SAC
A container woven from silk where a female spider lays her eggs.

STALK
To creep up on prey.

SUCKLE
When a baby animal drinks milk from its mother.

TEMPERATE
A place with mild weather—not too hot and not too cold.

TERRITORY
An area of land where one animal, or group of animals, lives and hunts.

VENOM
A liquid injected by an animal to kill its prey.

WEAN
When a baby stops drinking milk from its mother and eats solid food instead.

These websites have information about forests or their animals—or both!

- enchantedlearning.com/biomes
- globio.org/glossopedia/article.aspx?art_id=3
- kids.nationalgeographic.com/kids/animals
- nhptv.org/natureworks/nwep8c.htm
- sandiegozoo.org/animalbytes
- youtube.com/watch?v=f3YTvT3gqFI

Index

A
Africa, southern 5, 20–27
antennae 21
antlers 14, 15
Asia, southern 5, 6–13, 28–29
Australia 5

B
bats, vampire 16–17, 18
beaks 19, 25
bees 6–7, 8, 9
birds 18–19, 24–25, 26, 28
blood 15, 16, 17

C
camouflage 12, 14, 20
chameleons 22–23, 24
chicks 19, 24, 25
chimpanzees 5
claws 13, 18, 21
climbing 11, 13, 21, 23
consumers 4, 5
cubs 12, 13

D
deer 12, 14–15, 16
dogs, African wild 26–27

E
ears 15, 27
eggs 6, 8, 18, 20, 22, 24
equator 4
Europe 5
eyes 9, 11, 17, 18, 23, 25

F
fawns 14, 15

flowers 6, 7, 8, 9, 10
food chains 4, 5
food webs 28–29
fruit 10, 14, 29

H
hawks, red-tailed 18–19
hornbills 24–25
hunting 13, 18, 19, 23, 25, 27

I
insects 5, 6–7, 8, 9, 10, 20–21, 22, 24, 29

L
larvae 6, 7
leaves 4, 10, 11, 14, 15, 21
lynx 5

M
mammals 10–11, 12–13, 14–15, 16–17, 26–27, 28
mating 8, 14, 15, 16, 18, 22, 24, 26, 27
milk 10, 15, 16, 26
molting (shedding) 6, 21
monkeys, gray langur 10–11, 12, 28

N
nectar 6
nests 6, 18, 24
North America 4, 14–19
nymphs 20, 21

P
pill bugs 4

plants 4, 7, 14, 20, 29
predators 5, 8, 13, 15, 17, 22, 21, 23, 27
prey 5, 9, 12, 13, 17, 18, 23, 26
producers 4
pupae 7
pups 26, 27

R
rabbits 4
reptiles 22–23, 24

S
sounds 11, 15, 17, 25, 27
South America 4
spiders, white crab 8–9, 10, 29
stick insects 20–21, 22
Sun 4, 29

T
tails 15, 23, 27
teeth 13, 22, 27
tigers, Bengal 12–13, 28
toes 11, 19, 23
tongues 13, 23
trees 4, 11, 13, 14, 17, 18, 20, 23, 24

V
venom 7, 9